AF594815

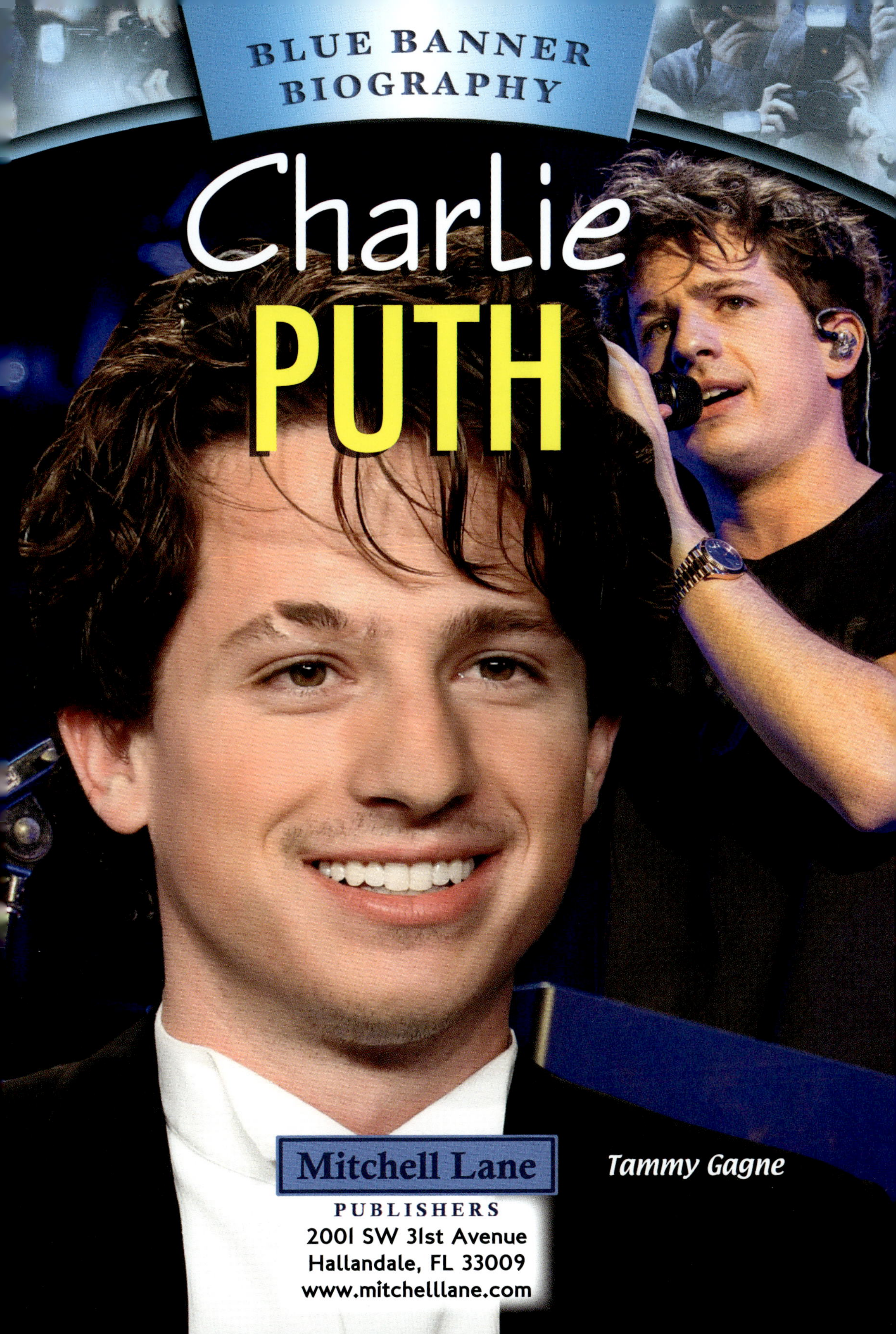
BLUE BANNER
BIOGRAPHY
Charlie
PUTH
Mitchell Lane
PUBLISHERS
2001 SW 31st Avenue
Hallandale, FL 33009
www.mitchelllane.com
Tammy Gagne

Printing 1 2 3 4 5 6 7 8 9

Blue Banner Biographies

5 Seconds of Summer
Aaron Judge
Abby Wambach
Adele
Alicia Keys
Allen Iverson
Ashanti
Ashlee Simpson
Ashton Kutcher
Avril Lavigne
Blake Lively
Blake Shelton
Bow Wow
Brett Favre
Britney Spears
CC Sabathia
Carrie Underwood
Carson Wentz
Charlie Puth
Chris Brown
Chris Daughtry
Christina Aguilera
Clay Aiken
Cole Hamels
Condoleezza Rice
Corbin Bleu
Daniel Radcliffe
David Ortiz
David Wright
Derek Hough
Derek Jeter
Drew Brees
Dwyane Wade
Eminem
Eve
Fergie
Flo Rida
Gwen Stefani
Hope Solo
Ice Cube
Jamie Foxx
James Harden
Jared Goff
Ja Rule
Jason Derulo
Jay-Z
Jennifer Hudson
Jennifer Lopez
Jessica Simpson
JJ Watt
J. K. Rowling
John Legend
Justin Berfield
Justin Timberlake
Kanye West
Kate Hudson
Keith Urban
Kelly Clarkson
Kenny Chesney
Ke$ha
Kevin Durant
Kristen Stewart
Lady Gaga
Lance Armstrong
Leona Lewis
Le'Veon Bell
Lindsay Lohan
LL Cool J
Ludacris
Luke Bryan
Maren Morris
Mariah Carey
Mario
Mary J. Blige
Mary-Kate and Ashley Olsen
Megan Fox
Miguel Tejada
Mike Trout
Nancy Pelosi
Natasha Bedingfield
Nicki Minaj
One Direction
Orianthi
Orlando Bloom
P. Diddy
Peyton Manning
Pharrell Williams
Pit Bull
Prince William
Queen Latifah
Robert Downey Jr.
Ron Howard
Russell Westbrook
Russell Wilson
Sean Kingston
Selena
Shia LaBeouf
Shontelle Layne
Soulja Boy Tell 'Em
Stephenie Meyer
Taylor Swift
T.I.
Timbaland
Tim McGraw
Toby Keith
Usher
Vanessa Anne Hudgens
The Weeknd
Will.i.am
Zac Efron

Library of Congress Cataloging-in-Publication Data
Names: Gagne, Tammy, author.
Description: Hallandale, FL : Mitchell Lane Publishers, [2019] | Series: Blue banner biographies | Includes bibliographical references and index.
Identifiers: LCCN 2017050211 | ISBN 9781680201789 (library bound) | ISBN 9781680201796 (ebook)
Subjects: LCSH: Puth, Charlie, 1991—Juvenile literature. Singers—United States—Biography—Juvenile literature.
Classification: LCC ML3930.P9 G34 2018 | DDC 782.42164092 [B] —dc23
LC record available at https://lccn.loc.gov/2017050211

ABOUT THE AUTHOR: Tammy Gagne has written more than 200 books for both adults and children. Her recent titles include several books about country music artists—including *Eric Church* and *Maren Morris*. She resides in northern New England with her husband and son.

PUBLISHER'S NOTE: The following story has been thoroughly researched and to the best of our knowledge represents a true story. While every possible effort has been made to ensure accuracy, the publisher will not assume liability for damages caused by inaccuracies in the data and makes no warranty on the accuracy of the information contained herein. This story has not been authorized or endorsed by Charlie Puth.

Blue Banner Biography

Charlie Puth is an unlikely pop star. It was his songwriting skills that led to his big break as a singer. His song "See You Again" beat out dozens of others when he submitted it to be played during an emotional scene in the 2015 movie Furious 7. *Little did he know then that he would be recording it with Wiz Khalifa.*

1 Hard Work Forever Pays

"Yes!" shouted Kyle as the last note of the song echoed from his portable keyboard. "I think it's done," he told his friend Jon, who was smiling as widely as Kyle. It had been a long day. But the boys hoped all their hard work would pay off. They had been writing songs together ever since they met two years earlier in the sixth grade. Now they were finally old enough to enter the Young Songwriters Competition. That was a contest sponsored by the music store where they had both taken piano lessons for even longer than they'd been friends.

The contest always attracted hundreds of entries. The winners got to make a high-quality demo of their song in the store's recording studio. Then it would be played on the weekly pop countdown of a local radio station. Several previous winners had sold their songs to successful artists. A couple had even gotten record contracts. Kyle and Jon wanted more than anything to follow in the footsteps of those talented songwriters.

"I think we have a shot with this one," Jon said. "We could actually have careers in the music business."

Charlie Puth never thought he would become a successful singer. He came to Los Angeles to try to make a living as a songwriter.

"You're dreaming," scoffed Kyle's older sister as she opened the fridge on the other side of the family's great room and grabbed a yogurt drink. The boys didn't realize that Marissa had been listening. She never had anything positive to say about their music—nor about anything else lately. "Do you realize what a longshot that is?" She had a white earbud in one ear while the other bud dangled below her elbow. The Wiz Khalifa song "See You Again" blared from the tiny speaker.

"We do know," Jon said. "But we've got just as good a shot as anyone else." As she rolled her eyes, he continued. "That song you're listening to was once a longshot as well. Charlie Puth wrote it for the movie *Furious 7*. More than a hundred other songwriters submitted songs to play during Paul Walker's final scene in the movie. But the producers chose his. That song is the reason why he is so successful today."

"That's interesting. You seem to know a lot about music," Marissa said as she glanced down at her phone on the other end of the headphones. "Who knows? Maybe you *will* win," she said. "I only heard the end of your song, but it wasn't terrible." Coming from Marissa, those words were high praise.

* * * *

Charlie Puth never thought he would become a successful singer. He came to Los Angeles to try to make a living as a songwriter. But when Atlantic Records and the producers of *Furious 7* chose his song for the film's soundtrack, they also asked him to sing some of the lyrics on the track. He has said that being asked to perform the song with Wiz Khalifa made that day the best of his young life.

Charlie had a special connection to the song. Actor Paul Walker died in a car accident in late 2013 during the

Charlie even got to attend the premiere of **Furious 7** *with Wiz Khalifa in Los Angeles in April of 2015.*

filming of *Furious 7*. His death left his family, friends, and millions of fans heartbroken. "See You Again" would be the song that played as the film said goodbye to Walker's character, Brian O'Conner. Sadly, Charlie had also lost a dear friend in a motor vehicle accident. This friend had always encouraged his musical career, assuring him that one day he would have a number-one song. His heartfelt support inspired Charlie to write "See You Again" in the friend's memory. And just as his friend had predicted, it reached the top spot on the Hot 100 Chart on April 25, 2015. It stayed there for three months.

Paul Walker

The song's music and lyrics came to Charlie quickly. It took him only ten minutes with DJ Frank E to write the chorus. Charlie loved the idea of the song being used to honor the late actor along with his friend. He hoped it would provide some comfort for people who had lost loved ones.

A Musical Genius

Charles Otto Puth, Jr. was born on December 2, 1991 in Rumson, New Jersey. He is the oldest of Charles and Debra Puth's three children. Charlie's younger siblings Stephen and Mikaela are fraternal twins. Charlie received his name from his father, who works as a real estate broker. His mother is a music teacher. She taught all three of her children how to play the piano. But Charlie showed the strongest interest in it and in music in general.

Charlie's fans have noticed that his right eyebrow has an unusual look. This is because a friend's Labrador Retriever attacked Charlie when he was two years old. The injury was so bad that Charlie almost died. Today, though, all that remains from the incident is a bare patch towards the end of his eyebrow. Before becoming aware of the story, many fans thought Charlie created the jagged look on purpose. Some fans have even imitated it by shaving their own eyebrows.

As a little boy, Charlie was always making noise. Toy musical instruments were among his favorite playthings. His mother has said that Charlie would spend hours in his bedroom with them. She started giving him piano lessons when he was just four. Six years later, he went on to study jazz at the School of Music and Drama in nearby Little Silver.

Both his family and his teachers realized early on that Charlie was a musical prodigy. He even had perfect pitch. That is the ability to identify and recreate the pitch of any musical note. Very few musicians have it. When his mother took him to the beach, he heard music in the wind and water. Charlie told her that the breeze sounded like a D-sharp, while a wave reminded him of a B-flat.

By the time he was in high school, Charlie spent his Saturdays at the Manhattan School of Music in New York City. While other boys his age were playing video games, he was studying jazz and classical music. His piano

Charlie is seen here performing at Michigan's Freedom Hill Amphitheater in 2016.

Mikaela and Stephen sometimes accompany their big brother to fun events, like the Los Angeles premiere of his single "Attention" in 2017.

teacher, Jim Josselyn, produced drum sounds on a computer so he could play along with them. This fascinated young Charlie, who soon realized that he wanted to be able to write and produce music himself.

Coming from New Jersey, Charlie had grown up near some famous pop musicians. Both Bruce Springsteen and Jon Bon Jovi live

Both his family and his teachers realized early on that Charlie was a musical prodigy.

just down the street from Charlie's family home. His mother knows Springsteen quite well. But jazz became the young prodigy's primary interest in the beginning. He also showed a tremendous talent for beatboxing, a practice that involves making drum sounds with the mouth.

Charlie was an enterprising young man. When he wasn't playing the piano for school or community productions, he was making money with his music. When he was in the sixth grade, he recorded his own holiday album called *Have a Merry Charlie Christmas*. After selling it door to door, he donated the $600 profit to a local church.

Bruce Springsteen

Charlie took his love of music seriously. Others noticed his enormous talent and dedication. While he was still in high school, he received a scholarship from the Berklee College of Music in Boston. While attending the prestigious school, he pursued a degree in music production and engineering.

Everything Charlie did always included some fun. While he was at Berklee, he and fellow student Emily Luther recorded their own

Charlie brought his father with him to the American Music Awards in 2015.

version of the song "Someone Like You," which had been made popular by Adele. They began the project as an entry for a contest for the best amateur cover of the song. Shortly after they uploaded their duet-style version to YouTube, it racked up an impressive number of views.

The view that mattered most, though, was from talk show host Ellen DeGeneres. After hearing Charlie and Emily's version of the song, Ellen invited them to appear on her show in 2011. When Charlie received the call from her producers, he thought it was a joke and hung up on them.

Ellen DeGeneres

Making a YouTube video with his friend Emily Luther led the pair to a television appearance.

Luckily, they called back. In addition to being a successful talk show host and comedian, Ellen is an avid music fan. She even has her own recording label called eleveneleven. About 15 million people watched the *Ellen* episode featuring Charlie and Emily. Among the viewers was an executive from Atlantic Records. At the time, though, Ellen signed the YouTube stars to eleveneleven. Charlie returned to the *Ellen* set to perform "See You Again" a few years later. He said that it was the least nervous he had ever felt before a performance because he felt like he was surrounded by family.

About 15 million people watched the Ellen episode featuring Charlie and Emily.

3 Writing, Recording, and Producing

After graduating from Berklee, Charlie moved to Los Angeles. Around the same time that Wiz Khalifa released "See You Again" in early 2015, Charlie had another new song. This one, "Marvin Gaye," honored the famous soul singer. It was a duet with fellow singer-songwriter Meghan Trainor. Her catchy debut song, "All About That Bass," had quickly turned her into a pop star the previous year. Meghan invited Charlie to join her on her MTrain tour that summer. By now, more and more people were taking notice of Charlie Puth. This opportunity would allow him to expand his fan base to an even greater extent.

By the time Charlie was ready to record his own full-length album, he had signed with Atlantic Records. But he didn't make the record in the usual way. After co-writing all 12 songs on *Nine Track Mind*, he recorded them in his bedroom. He didn't even use any studio equipment. He just played and recorded his music, with the help of several other talented

Writing and singing with other artists turned out to be a smart strategy.

songwriters and producers. He is especially proud of this fact and hopes it inspires other young people who want to make their own music.

Many producers who wanted to manage Charlie's career did not like that he wanted to be so involved in producing his own music. They warned him that he could not be a successful artist *and* a successful producer. They felt strongly that he needed to choose between these two passions. But Charlie felt strongly that he could do both well. He refused to work with the naysayers. He had worked tirelessly to learn about music production. He was determined to use that knowledge.

Writing and singing with other artists turned out to be a smart strategy. After working with Wiz Khalifa and Meghan Trainor, he went on to record a song with Lil Wayne. Charlie had grown up listening to Lil Wayne's music, so the chance to work with him was especially meaningful. Their song, "Nothing But

Lil Wayne

Trouble," was originally called "Instagram Models." It spoke to the shallow nature of posting photos on social media in hopes of racking up lots of likes.

Charlie's next duet was with pop star Selena Gomez. The two artists met while they were in London and hit it off immediately. In addition to sharing a love of music, they formed a real friendship. He got the idea for their song "We Don't Talk Anymore" when he was in Japan. Since all he had with him at the time was his cell phone, he used it to record the song. He continued working on it as he traveled, adding drums and vocals, before sending it to her. She loved it as soon as she heard it.

Charlie and Selena Gomez

He learned a lot from working with Selena—and from their friendship. As he told *Entertainment Tonight* in 2016, "She's very used to the spotlight, and I'm now kind of getting in that world, and I kind of got freaked out about it. She's a really good person that I can kind of turn to and ask for advice."

That same description also applies to his family.

To Charlie, family is the most important thing.

Charlie may be new to the professional music scene. But his success hasn't gone to his head. He knows that he wouldn't be where he is today without the love and support of his parents and siblings. He didn't grow up with money. And his family reminds him regularly that fame and money can go away quickly. To Charlie, family is the most important thing. When "See You Again" was nominated for three Grammy awards in 2016, Charlie chose to bring his mother as his date to the prestigious awards show. He also invited his brother and sister to move into his new home in Los Angeles with him. He even runs his music by his family because their opinions are so important to him.

When Charlie attended the 58th Grammy Awards in 2016, his mother Debra went as his date.

4 Changing the Culture

Many musicians and other famous people donate their time and money to favorite charities. They know that their fame can draw attention to important causes and help raise funds for them as well. In 2017, Charlie joined forces with the youth-oriented Hollister apparel firm (often shortened to HCo.) and STOMP Out Bullying. His fans who want to support the cause can purchase a blue T-shirt with "CHANGE THE CULTURE" on it. STOMP Out Bullying's goal is to create a world where people can be themselves while also being accepted by those around them. This cause is especially important to Charlie. He was a victim of bullying himself when he was younger.

Bullies often seek out people who are different and make fun of them. As a kid who found music in nearly every sound he heard, Charlie was definitely different. Some kids bullied him verbally when he talked about this ability. That might have caused him to stop exploring

Charlie's involvement in the STOMP Out Bullying campaign is more than just charity work for him. Many of his fans might be surprised to know that Charlie has been a victim of bullying himself.

his interest in music. But he chose to keep being himself when others were rude or abusive. When Charlie was younger, he dealt with bullying by finding positive things to do. If he was upset, he did things such as working out or going for a drive. He also found that just being alone for a while was enough to get focused on his music again. By finding healthy ways to cope with his feelings, he kept moving forward with his music, which

When Charlie was younger, he dealt with bullying by finding positive things to do.

ultimately helped him make it in the music business. He has had many other amazing experiences because of his involvement with music.

Although many people might assume that celebrities do not get bullied, this is not the case. People still single Charlie out and say mean things to him, sometimes quite publicly. But he has held onto his positive attitude through this new type of bullying. When someone continually left hateful comments on his Instagram page recently, he reached out to the person. Charlie learned that things were

Charlie also supports Stand Up To Cancer (SU2C). This charity raises money for cancer research, with a focus on getting the latest treatments to patients with this life-threatening illness.

Charlie performs during Z100's Jingle Ball 2016 at Madison Square Garden.

not going well in that person's life. Instead of striking back, he chose to be kind and try to help.

In addition to his fame, Charlie has found a way to use his talent to raise money for important charities. One of the things that Charlie and other popular musicians are best at is selling music. When artists donate even a small amount of the proceeds from a successful song to charity, everyone wins. Fans receive great music, and the charity receives much-needed funds.

In 2016, Charlie and several other popular performers recorded a holiday song to raise money for Robin Hood. This is an organization in New York City that helps fight homelessness and poverty by working with more than 200 programs in the city. Besides Charlie, the group included Joe Jonas' band DNCE, Fifth Harmony, and Hailee Steinfeld. It performed "Santa Claus is Coming to Town" at the annual Jingle Ball in Madison Square Garden. Fans of the artists could download the single, with 100 percent of the profits going directly to the cause.

Music is such as huge part of Charlie's life that he wants to make sure other young people who share his passion have the opportunity to learn more about it. So he became an ambassador for VH1's Save the Music Foundation. In 2016, the foundation donated 18 Casio Grand Hybrid pianos—worth $10,000 each—to schools around the United States. Charlie delivered the instruments personally. He remembers how his own school ditched its music program after the eighth grade. He didn't want that to happen to other young people who hear the same musical calling that he did.

Charlie enjoys helping other young people who want to pursue careers in music. He is seen here watching students at Boston's Josiah Quincy Upper School perform one of his songs at the VH1 Save The Music event in 2016.

5 The Gossip, the Truth, and the Future

When people become famous, the media often start to focus on their personal lives. Fans want to know as much as they can about their favorite artists. The press does its best to gather detailed information. All of a sudden, even simple things like hanging out with friends become subject matter for gossip blogs or magazine articles. In Charlie's case, the press has tried to link him to romances with several of his recording partners.

When Charlie performed with Meghan Trainor at the American Music Awards in 2015, they ended their song "Marvin Gaye" with an on-stage kiss. It prompted many questions about the relationship between the two singers. Fans wondered if they had become a couple while recording their song. But both singers denied that they were anything more than friends. They said that the kiss was simply part of the performance. Charlie has also been linked to Selena Gomez and Hailee Steinfeld. He has denied romantic relationships with both of those young women, too.

Charlie doesn't have much time for dating. He spends a lot of his time on a tour bus these days. In a

Charlie's performance with Meghan Trainor at the 2015 American Music Awards led to many questions about the relationship between the two musical artists.

recent interview, he said that he passes the down time by eating pizza and binge-watching his favorite television show, *Narcos*, on Netflix by himself. Charlie isn't against finding the right match, though. He has even shared the quality that is most important to him in the opposite sex: confidence. He likes people who believe in themselves. This quality matters more to him than what a young woman looks like. He has said that

Charlie doesn't have much time for dating. He spends a lot of his time on a tour bus these days.

he doesn't care if a girl's hair is purple, green, or another color—as long as she is confident.

Charlie is often rather unsure of his own decisions. He has joked that he likes the idea of finding someone who could help him decide which shirt to wear each day. He often changes several times before finding just the right one.

Charlie appeared on the *TODAY Show* in 2017. He was getting ready to release his second album, *Voicenotes*, which he produced himself. He told the show's hosts that the title relates to how often he used his phone's voice recording app while he was writing music for the album. "I'm really bad at writing music notes down," he said. "When I have an idea, I just record it on my phone and then I go to the studio and break it down."

The singer added that the album would reveal more about who he really is than *Nine Track Mind*. Although it was wildly successful, Charlie's first album was filled with love songs that other people encouraged him to write. While the songs meant something to him, he doesn't think they reflected his authentic self. He said the songs on the new album were inspired by darker times in his life, mistakes he made. He wants the world to know he is not perfect.

Although it was wildly successful, Charlie's first album was filled with love songs that other people encouraged him to write.

He released "Attention," the lead single for *Voicenotes* in April, 2017. By August, it had reached the number-5 spot on the Billboard Top 100. When he was writing the song, Charlie wanted to combine a good dance beat with a phrase that people often use with great emotion. When his fans hear the words "You just want attention," he wants them to feel something. He thinks that an emotional connection, along with the right dance beat, is the key to a hit record. Like his song "Nothing But Trouble," this one was also inspired by the social media platform. He got the idea for it while scrolling through photos.

Charlie is seen here performing on the Illuminate World Tour in 2017.

While his music may be moving in a darker direction, Charlie still just wants to make people happy with his music. He also likes the idea of getting people up and moving with his dance songs like "Attention." And he did just that as he spent the summer opening for his friend and fellow musician Shawn Mendes on his Illuminate World Tour. Charlie has said that he wants to release a new album every year. That is a lofty goal. It reflects how much the music world wants to keep hearing from this imperfect guy with perfect pitch.

1991 Charles Otto Puth is born on December 2.

1996 He starts taking piano lessons from his mother.

2001 Charlie enters the School of Music and Drama in Little Silver, New Jersey and is identified as a musical prodigy.

2011 A YouTube video of Charlie and a friend singing "Someone Like You" goes viral; Ellen DeGeneres invites him to appear on her show and later signs him to her record label eleveneleven.

2015 His song "See You Again" reaches the top of the Hit 100 chart and stays there three months; tours with Meghan Trainor.

2016 Charlie releases his album *Nine Track Mind*; "See You Again" is nominated for three Grammy awards; he is part of a concert that raises money for the charity Robin Hood.

2017 Charlie joins with Hollister for the STOMP Out Bullying campaign.

2018 Releases his second album, *Voicenotes*.

2016 *Nine Track Mind*
2017 *Voicenotes*

Charlie Puth, Official Website
http://www.charlieputh.com/

STOMP Out Bullying
http://www.stompoutbullying.org/

VH1 Save the Music Foundation
http://www.vh1savethemusic.org/

———. "Charlie Puth Tells How His Mom Found Out About His Supposed Relationship With Selena Gomez." Mix 104.1, April 6, 2016. http://mix1041.cbslocal.com/2016/04/06/salt-went-to-the-charlie-puth-concert-last-night/

———. "Hollister Co. Announces 2017 Ani-Bullying Campaign in Partnership with STOMP Out Bullying™ with Multi-Platinum, Multi-Grammy Nominated Recording Artist and Producer, Charlie Puth." Global News Wire, September 8, 2017. https://globenewswire.com/news-release/2017/09/08/1116953/0/en/Hollister-Co-Announces-2017-Anti-Bullying-Campaign-in-Partnership-With-STOMP-Out-Bullying-and-Multi-Platinum-Multi-Grammy-Nominated-Recording-Artist-and-Producer-Charlie-Puth.html

———. "Who We Fund." Robin Hood. https://www.robinhood.org/programs/who-we-fund/#all

———. "Wiz Khalifa." Billboard. http://www.billboard.com/artist/431494/wiz-khalifa/chart

PHOTO CREDITS: Cover, p. 1—Jon Kopaloff/Stringer/WireImage/Getty Images, (background) ZUMA Press, Inc./Alamy Stock Photo; p. 4—Eugene Gologursky/Stringer/Getty Images; p. 7—Michael Kovacz/Stringer/Getty Images; p. 8—Fernanda Calfat/Contributor/Getty Images; p. 10—Scott Legato/Contributor/Getty Images; p. 11—Tibrina Hobson/Stringer/Getty Images; p. 12—JDawnInk/Getty, p. 12—Bill Ebbesen/cc-by-sa 3.0; p. 13—Jordan Strauss/Invision/AP, ronpaulrevolt2008/cc-by-sa 2.0; p. 14—Jason Kempin/Staff/Getty Images; p. 16—Megan Elice Meadows/cc-by-sa 2.0; p. 17—Kevin Mazur/Contributor/Getty Images; p. 18—Jeff Vespa/Contributor/Getty Images; p. 20—Abercrombie & Fitch Management Co./GlobeNewswire; p. 21—Kevork Djansezian/Stringer/Getty Images; p. 22—Mike Coppola/Staff/Getty Images; p. 23—Scott Eisen/Stringer/Getty Images; p. 25—Jeff Kravitz/AMA2015/Contributor/Getty Images; p. 27—Steve Jennings/Contributor/Getty Images. Artwork/freepik.

Bell, Sadie. "Charlie Puth Reveals Title of His New Album, Performs 'Attention' on 'Today': Watch." *Billboard*, June 30, 2017. http://www.billboard.com/articles/columns/pop/7850114/charlie-puth-today-show-performance-new-album-title-interview-video

Berger, Rod. "Famed Singer Charlie Puth and VH1 Save the Music Foundation Team Up to Deliver Pianos to Students." LinkedIn.com, July 27, 2016. https://www.linkedin.com/pulse/famed-singer-charlie-puth-vh1-team-up-deliver-pianos-rod-berger-psyd

Buffum, Joanna. "Charlie Puth, Rumson's Pop Prodigy. *New Jersey Monthly*, January 12, 2016. https://njmonthly.com/articles/jersey-living/jersey-celebrities/charlie-puth-rumsons-pop-prodigy/

Charlton, Lauretta. "What to Expect on the Solo Debut From Charlie Puth, Pop's Duet Partner Du Jour." *Vulture*, December 2, 2015. http://www.vulture.com/2015/12/charlie-puth-talks-debut-album-nine-track-mind.html

Cirisano, Tatiana. "Anatomy of a Hit: Charlie Puth on the Runaway Success of 'Attention.'" *Billboard*, August 11, 2017. http://www.billboard.com/articles/columns/pop/7889744/charlie-puth-attention-interview

Ferber, Taylor. "Charlie Puth Is Ready For A Girlfriend & He Knows Exactly What He's Looking For." Bustle, September 12, 2016. https://www.bustle.com/articles/183299-charlie-puth-is-ready-for-a-girlfriend-he-knows-exactly-what-hes-looking-for

Ferrer, William Robert. "There's more to Charlie Puth than love songs." *Seattle Times*, July 5, 2017. https://www.seattletimes.com/entertainment/music/theres-more-to-charlie-puth-than-love-songs/

Highfill, Samantha. "Charlie Puth talks writing 'See You Again' for Paul Walker's goodbye." *Entertainment Weekly*, April 7, 2015. http://ew.com/article/2015/04/07/charlie-puth-see-you-again-paul-walker/

Mansfield, Brian. "Jazzy songwriter Puth: We'll 'See You Again.'" *USA Today*, May 31, 2015. https://www.usatoday.com/story/life/music/ontheverge/2015/05/31/charlie-puth-see-you-again-on-the-verge/27773703/

McIntyre, Hugh. "Charlie Puth Has The Number One Song in the Country… So Who Is He?" *Forbes*, April 23, 2015. https://www.forbes.com/sites/hughmcintyre/2015/04/23/charlie-puth-has-the-number-one-song-in-the-country-so-who-is-he/#11dedb923bae

McNamara, Brittney. "Charlie Puth Says He Was Severely Bullied in High School." *Teen Vogue*, September 2, 2016. https://www.teenvogue.com/story/charlie-puth-bullying-high-school

Nelson, Jeff. "Selena Gomez and Charlie Puth Are Nothing 'Other Than Friends,' Source Tells PEOPLE." *People*, March 30, 2016. http://people.com/celebrity/selena-gomez-not-dating-charlie-puth-stars-nothing-other-than-friends-source/

Park, Andrea. "Who is Charlie Puth? 6 things you need to know." CBS News, November 23, 2015. https://www.cbsnews.com/news/who-is-charlie-puth-6-things-you-need-to-know/

Russian, Ale. "DNCE, Fifth Harmony, Hailee Steinfeld, Team Up to Help the Homeless at New York Jingle Ball." *People*, December 8, 2016. http://people.com/music/dnce-fifth-harmony-hailee-steinfeld-help-homeless-new-york-jingle-ball/

Schillaci, Sophie. "Exclusive: Charlie Puth Reveals the Crazy Story Behind His Selena Gomez Collaboration, 'We Don't Talk Anymore.'" *Entertainment Tonight*, January 19, 2016. http://www.etonline.com/news/180401_exclusive_charlie_puth_reveals_the_crazy_story_behind_his_selena_gomez_collaboration

Trust, Gary. "Charlie Puth's 'Attention' Ascends to No. 1 on Pop Songs Chart." *Billboard*, August 28, 2017. http://www.billboard.com/articles/columns/chart-beat/7942257/charlie-puth-attention-no-1-pop-songs-chart

Vain, Madison. "Breaking Big: Charlie Puth." *Entertainment Weekly*, April 24, 2015. http://ew.com/article/2015/04/24/breaking-big-charlie-puth/

Weist, Brianna. "Charlie Puth Explains Why He and Meghan Trainor Made Out at the AMAs." *Teen Vogue*, November 25, 2015. https://www.teenvogue.com/story/charlie-puth-explains-ama-makeout-with-meghan-trainor

INDEX